Miff and the Long Nap

By Sascha Goddard

Miff likes to have long naps with Ted in her lap.

Joff wants to play.

Flap, flap!

"The sun is up, Miff!"
Joff yaps.
"Let's have some fun!"

Miff still naps.

Tap, tap!

"Miff, I have a map!"

Joff yaps.

"We can snap up some fish."

But Miff will not get up.

"You can put on
my best cap, Miff!" Joff yaps.

Miff **still** naps.

Joff flaps his fins.

"I can not snap Miff
out of her nap.
We will not get to play."

"Come on, you sad chap!"
Miff yells.

He winks at Joff.

"Where is the map?"

Tap, tap.

Joff claps his fins.

Clap, clap.

CHECKING FOR MEANING

1. What does Joff have to help him find fish? *(Literal)*

2. How does Joff describe the cap he offers Miff? *(Literal)*

3. Is the story set during the day or at night? How do you know? *(Inferential)*

EXTENDING VOCABULARY

naps	Look at the word *naps*. What does it mean? How is a nap different from a sleep?
yells	What does it mean if someone *yells*? What are some other words that mean the same as *yells*?
winks	Look at the word *winks*. What is the base of this word? Find three other words in the story that end in *s*.

MOVING BEYOND THE TEXT

1. What is it like where seals and polar bears live?

2. Would you like to live where there is snow and ice? Why or why not?

3. Where is a good place to have a nap?

4. What are some good ways to wake someone up?

SPEED SOUNDS

at	an	ap	et	og	ug

ell	ack	ash	ing

PRACTICE WORDS

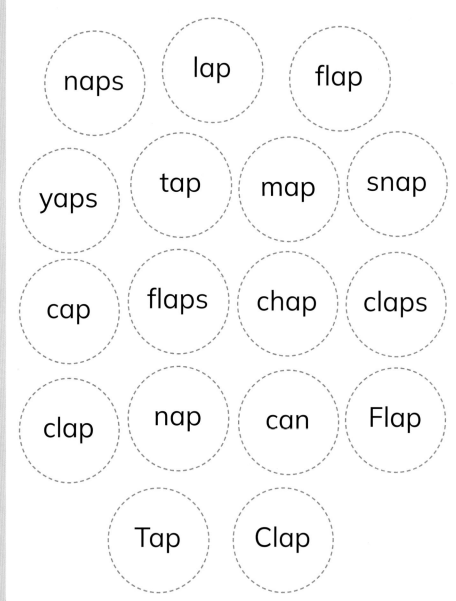

naps

lap

flap

yaps

tap

map

snap

cap

flaps

chap

claps

clap

nap

can

Flap

Tap

Clap